Stop Enabling
Drug Addicts
and Alcoholics

Enabling an addict is a harmful type of behavior if it keeps the addict from facing the consequences of their choices. Consequences are necessary to change bad behavior.

AUDREY PHILLIPS COX

The following are links if the book is being read on a digital device:

APCWriter & Publisher for updates:

www.facebook.com/writerpublisher

My APCWriter website for miscellaneous information:

www.apc-writer.com

My Amazon Author Page to purchase books::

www.amazon.com/author/apc-writer

CONTENTS:

1. NOTE FROM THE AUTHOR
2. DEFINITION OF AN ENABLER
3. DEFINING ADDITION
4. PERSONALITY OF AN ADDICT
5. CHEMICAL EFFECT ON BRAIN OF AN ADDICT
6. PERSONALITY OF AN ENABLER
7. AN ENABLER'S PRAYER
8. JOSH'S STORY – ADDICT
9. READ TRUE STORIES
10. MARSHA'S STORY – ENABLER
11. MARIE'S STORY – ADDICT
12. SUSAN'S STORY – ENABLER
13. CHARLIE'S STORY – ADDICT
14. GWEN'S STORY – ENABLER
15. TOM'S STORY – ADDICT
16. BEATRICE'S STORY – ENABLER
17. RACHEL'S STORY – ADDICT
18. MICHAEL'S STORY - ENABLER
19. MATT'S STORY - ADDICT
20. CONNIE'S STORY – ENABLER
21. PAULA'S STORY – ADDICT
22. HELPFUL WEBSITES TO VISIT
OTHER BOOKS WRITTEN BY AUTHOR

NOTE FROM THE AUTHOR

I have written this book to hopefully "wake up" some well-meaning people who are sometimes referred to as "codependent/enablers" of an alcoholic or a drug addict.

Many enablers cannot understand how "helping" a person in need can sometimes be harmful behavior in that it keeps an addict from maturing into responsible individuals by not allowing them to suffer the consequences of their behavior. Consequences serve to change a person's behavior.

While the beginning pages of this book deals with the psychology and medical aspects of addictive behavior, the remainder of the book has "true" stories of addict's and enabler's experiences living as an addict or an enabler who tries to help an addict in need. The names have been changed to provide privacy and prevent embarrassment for the characters in these stories. Some stories are told in "first-person" POV and others in "third person" POV, according to how I have received or learned of the story.

While this book is not affiliated with Al-Anon, Nar-Anon, or any organization that deals with codependent/enabling behavior, I have a similar goal: to provide information and support for anyone suffering from the negative consequences of "enabling" an alcoholic or drug addict.

I have deliberately kept the pages in this book to a minimum because I feel that most people do not want to wade through a lot of medical terms, that only medical people can comprehend, to obtain some coveted information about "enabling behavior."

What does co-dependency mean? For whatever reason, a person who needs to be "needed" couples up with an "addict" who needs someone to help them survive their addiction, and this creates a co-dependency relationship. However, I will use "enabling" throughout this book.

I would like to encourage the reader to seek out articles and other books by authors that contain additional information to broaden his/her knowledge about "enabling behavior." Knowledge is a powerful tool in dealing with this complex problem that is affecting so many people in the world.

While I have a Bachelor of Science Degree in Nursing and some clinical experience in dealing with addicts and also dealing with addicts in my private life, I have done some extensive online research for this book.

I have copied and pasted valuable information from some websites into this book. However, the websites have far more information than I can quote in this book, so I encourage the reader to explore the websites in depth.

In publishing the "true" stories, I have taken my writer's "artistic license" to re-word the stories slightly for clarity while preserving the fundamental truth and meaning of their words. I have included "addict" stories for "enablers" to see how an addict thinks once they are ensnared by their addiction and vice-versa why an addict uses an enabler. Hopefully, these real stories will turn on a light bulb and evoke a moment where the reader says to him/herself, "Ah-ha!"

DEFINITION OF AN ENABLER

As per **www.merriam-webster.com**: *"One that enables another to achieve an end; ESPECIALLY: one who enables another to persist in self-destructive behavior (as substance abuse) by providing excuses or by helping that individual avoid the consequences of such behavior."*

Helping (enabling) a person too much (an over-the-top type of support) inhibits the person's ability to develop strong qualities that include moral values, the capacity to feel compassion, good survival skills, and more. Sometimes, a person must be challenged to survive hardships to develop an inner strength that will keep them from turning into an addict.

Hopefully, through the information provided in this book, plus the "true stories" of both addicts and enablers contained in this book, enablers will "wake up" to the fact that helping an addict too much is a dysfunctional form of behavior. When an addict is provided too much support by a misguided but well-meaning enabler, it diminishes an addict's motivation to give up their addiction and learn how to survive on their own; therefore, it hinders them from developing into a mature and responsible person.

As per **www.psychcentral.com**: *"Enabling prevents the person engaging in destructive behavior from feeling or experiencing the consequences of his own actions, says Psych Central. This can be extremely damaging as negative consequences are usually the driving force behind change. Enabling actually prevents the person from changing and can prolong the duration of an addiction or similar illness."*

At this point, I want to remind readers that alcoholics and drug addicts are ordinary people who never set out to be addicts. They may find themselves unable to cope with the many stresses encountered in life: a bad marriage, a demanding boss, an unruly, rebellious teenager, financial problems, and more.

One or two drinks may temporarily help them to deal with their problems but wake up one day and find themselves ensnared by a chemical that has taken over their lives. In some cases, they may turn to drugs or alcohol for no reason at all. Before judging someone's addiction, one should consider: *"But for the grace of God, there goes I."*

Once a person becomes an addict, their attitude and outlook on life usually changes dramatically; therefore, their behavior negatively affects everyone around them, especially family and friends who have a close relationship with him/her.

It is said that one addict negatively impacts the lives of at least ten other people, sometimes causing irreparable psychological damage that hinders the enabler(s) from achieving their optimum level of well-being. It 's hard for someone with an enabling personality to see how providing help can be harmful to an addict.

In obtaining my BSN in nursing degree, one of my semesters were allotted to learning about psychiatric nursing, including addictions. Post-graduation, I also acquired some experience in the psychiatric field, including addictions, by working in a couple of mental facilities.

Although I had a "book knowledge" about addictions and codependency, I have spent many years enabling several addicts in my personal life. I couldn't seem to translate this book knowledge into action regarding my dysfunctional behavior. In other words, I could "talk the talk," but I could not "walk the walk." However, after many wasted years, I have finally seen the light, and I am now a recovered "enabler."

Before I move on to the "true stories" of both addicts and enablers, I feel the need to provide some fundamental information regarding an addict's personality, how the chemicals affect their brain, and explain why it is hard for them to give up their addiction. I will write about the characteristics of enablers who aid addicts in their addiction.

It is clear: an addict needs to give up their drug-of-choice to become a responsible person.

It is not-so-clear: an enabler needs to see the fine line between appropriate "helping" and dysfunctional "enabling."

As per **www.alcoholrehab.com**: *"Enabling is one of the key aspects of addiction and substance abuse. Many people who struggle with addiction find that they have a close relationship with a person who enables them to deny that they have a problem with drugs or alcohol. This dysfunctional relationship also allows them to ignore and be **disconnected from the consequences** of their behavior An enabler will provide emotional and financial support, help them to hide their addiction, fund their addiction and even make excuses for their problems. The addict knows that there is always someone there to help them, even if they permit the most hurtful, painful and even criminal acts."*

DEFINING ADDICTION

An excerpt from The American Society of Addictive Medicine, which applies to all addictions including codependency:

As per **www.asamcriteria.org**: *"The addiction is characterized by impairment in behavioral control, craving, inability to consistently abstain, and diminished recognition of significant problems with one's behaviors and interpersonal relationships. Like other chronic diseases, addiction can involve cycles of relapse and remission. Without treatment or engagement in recovery activities, addiction is progressive and can result in disability or premature death."*

What are the common traits of an addict? Studies have shown that there are no behavioral characteristics that distinctly describe an addict, but there are some common characteristics that thread throughout most addictions. Some of these traits are noticeable from early childhood and usually becomes visible during the teenage years.

PERSONALITY OF AN ADDICT

Some of the following characteristic behaviors can be noted in the personality of an addict.

As per **www.wikipedia.org**: *"People that face this issue are currently defined to have a "brain disease" as promoted by the* **National Institute on Drug Abuse** *(www.drugabuse.gov) and other authorities. People who experience addictive personality disorders typically act on impulses and cannot deal with* **delayed gratification**.[5] *At the same time, people with this type of personality tend to believe that they do not fit into societal norms and therefore, acting on* **impulses**, *deviate from conformity to rebel. People with addictive personalities are very sensitive to* **emotional stress**. *They have trouble handling situations that they deem frustrating, even if the event is for a very short duration. The combination of low* **self-esteem**, **impulsivity** *and low tolerance for stress causes these individuals to have frequent* **mood swings** *and often suffer from some sort of* **depression**. *A coping mechanism to deal with their conflicting personality* *becomes their addiction and the addiction acts as something that the person can control when they find it difficult to control their personality traits."*

An addict may only exhibit one or more of these types of behavior, and people who possess many of them may not become an addict.

1. Impulsive
2. Selfish
3. Manipulative
4. Lies easily
5. Critical
6. Plays the victim role
7. Sociopathic tendencies
8. May sometimes appear to have two personalities
9. Possesses low self-esteem
10. Over-reacts to stress
11. Suffers from depression or anxiety
12. Seeks sensational activities
13. Resists conforming to rules and regulations
14. Dependent personality but insists on independence
15. Denies being an addict

(handwritten note: personality of an addict)

Experts agree that only excessive participation in any activity can be defined as an addiction. In other words, the desire for their *drug-of-choice* must become an obsession. The addiction may be classified into two general categories based on the consequences suffered by the addict and how it affects the people around them. Many people may disagree with my categories, and that's okay:

1. **Soft addictions:** smoking, gambling, over-spending, eating, surfing the Internet, and other excessive activities

2. **Hard addictions:** alcoholic, drug addictions (due to chemicals involved)

There are two general types of addicts:

1. **Functioning addict:** An addict that can maintain a normal or almost normal lifestyle; can work and provide a living for themselves and their immediate family members. Nothing appears amiss to others during social engagements. Many of them possess passive-aggressive personalities. However, their behavior impacts their closely-held relationships.

2. **Non-functioning addict:** An addict that cannot maintain a normal lifestyle; cannot work or engage in normal social activities or provide a living for

themselves. Their behavior is out-of-control. Most of them possess overt-aggressive personalities.

CHEMICAL EFFECT ON BRAIN OF ADDICT

As per **www.venturarecoverycenter.com/drugs-alcohol-affect-brain:** *"The limbic system is not the only part of the brain affected by prolonged drug or alcohol abuse. The frontal lobe of the brain also suffers. It shrinks and loses its ability to function properly. This part of the brain regulates decisions, choices, and the ability to know the difference between right and wrong. When the frontal lobe is not working as it should, you cannot control the impulse to drink or take drugs. Ironically the essential part of the brain you would use to change your harmful habits is impaired by those harmful habits and unable to make the proper decisions."*

As a result, the ability to feel any pleasure is reduced. The person feels flat, lifeless, and depressed, and is unable to enjoy things that once brought pleasure. Now the person needs drugs just to bring dopamine levels up to normal, and more of the drug is needed to create a dopamine flood, or "high"—an effect known as "tolerance."

This factor explains why some people may increase their drug/alcohol ingestion to continue searching for the "reward system" but may eventually lead to drug/alcoholic addiction.

The effect alcohol/drugs have on the brain:

When a person drinks alcohol or ingests drugs, they experience a feeling of pleasurable, and they cannot obtain this high-level of euphoria without the aid of alcohol or drugs. Chronic use can seriously affect the brain.

The difference between the recreational and chronic use of alcohol or drugs:

Infrequent recreational use will not do serious long-term damage to the brain, but chronic users may suffer serious consequences such as attention deficit problems, memory loss, and difficulty in learning. Infrequent users can usually sustain a stable lifestyle while chronic users become more and more unstable in all of their ways.

However, excessive recreational use of either chemical can alter a person's personality and can negatively impact his/her close relationships.

What happens once the alcohol or drugs are consumed:

After ingesting alcohol or drugs, there are complex functions that take place in the brain. There are neurons, synapses, and neurotransmitters located in the brain that processes the chemicals. While five neurotransmitters are affected by the chemicals, two of them have a profound effect on the brain: Dopamine and Serotonin which occurs naturally in the brain.

Dopamine produces the sensation of pleasure and Serotonin produces a sense of well-being. The alcohol/drugs affect the body's natural mechanism for producing Dopamine and Serotonin in the synaptic gaps of the brain. Drugs/alcohol elevates the normal levels which create the euphoria that the addict desires.

With chronic use, an addict's brain is affected by neuro-adaptive processes (adjustment to the chemicals) within the circuits of the central nervous system and produces less of the neurotransmitters; then the brain becomes dependent on drugs/alcohol to produce even mild feelings of pleasure and well-being. This is why an addict must gradually increase the amount of drugs/alcohol they ingest to obtain a high.

What happens when the brain is denied alcohol/drugs:

When an alcoholic or drug addict is denied alcohol/drugs, the natural mechanisms of the brain that produces pleasure and feelings of well-being can be impacted and will not function properly, causing Dopamine and Serotonin to be depleted, blunted or obliterated. In other words, when alcohol or drugs have chronically provided a person with a pseudo type of "reward system," this causes the brain to adapt to the change and decrease its natural production of Dopamine and Serotonin. If the chemicals are suddenly and completely withdrawn, the body goes through a traumatic change, and an addict will go into delirium tremors.

Delirium Tremors:

A person can undergo delirium tremors during withdrawal from alcohol or drugs. Delirium tremors are commonly referred to as the DTs. During this dangerous experience, the addict experiences severe symptoms of paranoia, anxiety, depression, and restlessness. If the addict attempts to go "cold turkey," due to his/ her inability to obtain their drug-of-choice or their conscious decision to come off the alcohol/drugs without treatment, it can be fatal. The withdrawal experience should be done in a hospital setting.

This is also the period in the withdrawal experience that an addict is tempted to give in to their terrible symptoms and may return to the chemical that will alleviate his/her terrible symptoms. Therefore, a vicious and chronic cycle of dependence begins, and this makes it hard for an addict to give up their addiction.

Once the drugs and alcohol are no longer in a person's system, the brain once again recognizes the need to provide Dopamine and Serotonin. However, this process does not happen overnight.

An alcoholic or drug addict "slowly" becomes an addict, and the brain slowly adjusts to the impact that drugs and alcohol have on the brain and starts shutting down the natural production of Dopamine and Serotonin. So, when the brain "wakes up" to the fact that it needs to produce a sufficient amount of Dopamine and Serotonin, it is also a "slow" process for a person's body to return to a normal state of being. This is why an addict has to fight so hard to resist "falling off the wagon" and are vulnerable to relapsing into their addiction again.

There may be other issues going on in the brain:

There may be mental health issues that further complicate a person's addiction. Chronic depression, Borderline Personality Disorder, Bipolar Disorder, and other diagnoses may play a major role in the process of becoming an addict. These psychiatric problems or neurotic tendencies must be considered when trying to rehabilitate an addict.

There may be a spiritual, moral compass missing in their lives. Some famous celebrities who are addicts have money, fame, and the adoration of millions. Why do they need a chemical in their bloodstream to make them happy?

You cannot simply tell an addict to...

Straighten up and fly right and expect them to do so, not after they have become a full-blown addict. An addict cannot be forced to give up his/her addiction but must make up his/her mind and truly desire to accept help from God and/or a professional to conquer their dependence on drugs. The addict knows that it will be very hard for them to overcome their addiction, and with their depleted "coping mechanisms," it hard for them to consider undertaking such a drastic decision.

PERSONALITY OF AN ENABLER

Without help from others, a full-blown addict has difficulty sustaining his/her addiction. If it were possible to eliminate well-meaning people who go overboard in helping addicts to survive, there would be fewer addicts in the world. Once a dysfunctional addict is denied help in obtaining food, shelter, and the other necessities of life, and they are forced to face the consequences of their addiction, they only have two choices: give up their addiction and make an effort to provide the necessities of life for themselves...or die.

As per **www.wikipedia.com:** *"Enabling can tend to prevent psychological **growth** in the person being enabled, and can contribute to negative symptoms in the enabler. Therapist Darline Lancer writes, "Stopping enabling isn't easy. Nor is it for the faint of heart. Aside from likely pushback and possible retaliation, you may also fear the consequences of doing nothing. For instance, you may fear your [addict] husband will lose his job...You may be afraid the addict may have an auto accident, or worse, die or commit suicide."*[5] *The* *parent may allow the addicted adult child to live at home without helping with chores, and be **manipulated** by the child's excuses, emotional attacks, and threats of self-harm."*

This why so many addicts wind up as homeless people on the streets, and sometimes they die on the streets. Most well-meaning people cannot bear to see an addict self-destruct. However, in their effort to help an addict, it creates a dysfunctional relationship between them. This behavior is especially prevalent amongst family members.

A codependent (enabling) person is very sensitive to the needs of others, and some might say that they are addicted to helping people in trouble. Many codependent/enablers need to be needed. Sometimes, this addiction is so strong the codependent will inadvertently cause the other person to continue to be needy.

The word "enabler" is another word that is commonly used for a codependent person, and I will primarily use that word in this book. A person with this type of personality sees themselves as the only person who can help someone by trying to be *Mr/Ms Fix-it;* sometimes they try to fix someone who does not need to be fixed.

Enabling includes behavior, thoughts, and feelings that go way beyond the usual care-taking or self-sacrificing. Codependency does not refer to all caring behavior or feelings, but only those that are excessive to an unhealthy degree.

One or more characteristics of an enabler:

1. Well-intentioned but misguided
2. Needs to be needed
3. Constantly in search of acceptance
4. Has control issues
5. Excessively preoccupied with other's needs
6. Denies being an enabler
7. Low self-esteem
8. Overly compliant to rules and regulations
9. Excessive care-taking or sacrificing
10. Often takes the role of a martyr
11. Sees themselves as victims
12. Tolerates abusive marriages and relationships
13. Seems to attract abusive people/situations

An enabler should ask themselves the following three questions:

Is this relationship destructive to my sense of well-being?

Love does make one selfless at times to make the other person in the relationship happy. One might say, "I like/love this person so much that I am willing to give a lot." But a person should not destroy themselves in the process of trying to make another person happy. If so, something is wrong

What price am I paying for my self-sacrificing ways toward this person?

If someone is always putting themselves last, that is not a healthy way to live. They must evaluate their behavior and change their dysfunctional approach to life.

Am I the only one truly trying to improve this relationship?

When only one person is putting forth any real effort, while the other person seems to be oblivious to the consequences of their bad behavior, then it is time for the codependent person to wake up to what is happening in their relationship.

Overt enabling behavior: This behavior is visible, such as providing shelter, food, and money to a person who should be providing for themselves. The enabler views this as being compassionate and helpful to an addict.

Passive enabling behavior: This behavior includes maintaining silence in the face of mental or physical abuse or other destructive behavior. For many reasons, the enabler fails to confront bad behavior. Sometimes, the enabler remains silent because they know it will only bring more abuse down upon their heads.

Many codependents will deny that they are an enabler. "I'm not codependent. It is just that I love them so much that I want to help them. I am afraid that they cannot get along without me. What will happen to them if I don't help?"

It is difficult for an enabler to see that helping an addict is harmful, especially if it is a loved one. Of course, some support is healthy, but when the addict is helped so much that they are no longer able to take care of themselves, or loses the motivation to do so, it then becomes unhealthy assistance.

When an addict is no longer furnished food, shelter, or money for necessities, they are then forced with the option of looking for a job or living on the streets. Sometimes, the cold reality of "living on the streets" wakes them up and they begin to face the consequences of their behavior. However, the longer they survive as an addict, with the help of others, the less they care when they wind up on the streets.

Once they hit the streets, they become street-wise in the ways of survival. This is why an enabler needs to stop helping an addict in the early stages of their addiction before it is too late. Some people will argue that it is never too late. However, people die on the streets every day.

Many times, codependency begins in a dysfunctional family. Children learn to compensate for the inappropriate behavior of one or more parent/sibling. Growing up, they have difficulty determining what is normal and what is considered acceptable behavior. Many of the children develop a need to *fix the problems* going on in the family. This is the basic personality of an enabler.

An enabler will call into work for an addict, make excuses for them, clean up problems caused by the addict, provide shelter and sustenance, and refuse to force the person to take responsibility for their behavior. Thinking that they are helping, in reality, they are not helping but are harming the addict. Rescuing an addict hinders them from healthy psychological growth.

People who suffer from codependency (enabling behavior) are more likely to stay in bad marriages, stressful jobs, unhappy relationships, and even attract abuse from others. The excessive need to *fix* people and to be *needed* drives their behavior. By developing unhealthy relationships, a codependent person is likely to become an addict themselves.

Enabling behavior covers far more than just dealing with addictions. Enablers want to fix all kinds of problems, not just relating to addicts, and not only in their own lives but in the lives of others. They are usually "positive thinking" people who want to make things better for everyone in life.

An enabler should go to Al-Anon, Nar-Anon, or other meetings of this type, where they can share their story and gain some insight into their codependent personalities by listening to the stories of other enablers. It can be a win-win situation, in that both the enabler and the addict will benefit from the effort.

As stated earlier, I include some "true" stories of both addicts and enablers in this book. In an Al-Anon, Nar-Anon, or some meeting dealing with the negative effects of enabling an addict, a codependent/enabler is required to concentrate on their behavior and avoid trying to understand the behavior of the addict in their lives.

I agree with their approach, but I am taking a slightly different approach to help an "enabler" see themselves as others see them. By reading a wide variety of different stories, told to me by both addicts and enablers; hopefully, it will enlighten the reader about addictions and codependency/enabling behavior.

After reading the Enabler's Prayer, the "true stories" of both addicts and enablers who have suffered from their choices; hopefully, the reader will see how their "helping" can sometimes be described as "enabling."

AN ENABLER'S PRAYER
by Audrey Phillips Cox

God grant me the wisdom

To know when to help someone in need

But to know the difference between

Helping and enabling

So that I will not hinder anyone

From facing the consequences of their actions

Or learning how to take care of themselves

Even when hardships plague them

So that they can grow and mature into successful people

To fulfill the plan that You have for their lives.

READ TRUE STORIES

OF

ADDICTS AND ENABLERS

Educate yourself! Read the following stories, alternating between addicts and enabler's stories; the addicts telling their experience in dealing with alcohol or drugs and how they respond to people who go out of their way to help them when they have spiraled downward to the point they can't help themselves.

When addicts need help to provide the necessities of life, "too much help" hinders them from suffering from the consequences of their addiction. It is said that suffering consequences is the only thing that will create change in an addict's behavior.

JOSH'S STORY – AN ADDICT

I am a recovering addict from both drugs and alcohol. When I entered high school, drugs were rampant, and I started doing drugs when I was fourteen. I am now fifty years old and have just begun to realize how I have wasted the best years of my life, spent in a blur of addiction.

Since I was raised by good, church-going parents, I had a good life and had no excuse for my addiction. Once I started taking drugs, I found that I could not turn back. They helped me to fit in with the other kids at school, and when I didn't fit in, it numbed me so that I did not care. As a teenager, I thought I had a lot of problems. Now, I realize how trivial they were in comparison to the problems I now face every day. Nevertheless, from that time until recently, I took the drugs to temporarily escape from the harsh realities of the real world.

My parents finally caught on to my drug habit. They were very disappointed, but I didn't care because the drugs diminished my guilty feelings. My father tried to talk to me, and I would agree with him, then as soon as I could, I purchased more drugs. It came increasingly easy to lie to my parents. My father would punish me, but it did no good. My attitude was that he was not going to tell me what to do. In other words, I became a rebellious teenager. My mother would interfere and try to convince my father that he was too hard on me.

In spite of myself, with some pushing from my father, I graduated from high school. During the graduation service, I was high on drugs. My father was livid. My mother was sad but took up for me when my father showed extreme disapproval with my behavior.

After graduation, I went to work in the construction field for a local contractor. At that time, the chemicals had not damaged my brain, and without trying very hard, I instinctively caught on to the mechanics of building a house. I have never been lazy, and I excelled in my job.

Later, when my boss started building high-rise commercial buildings, reading the complex blue-prints and supervising men to accomplish our goal was also easy for me. I don't have a lot of things to be proud of in my life, but I can look back on those days and be proud of some of the buildings that the company built under my supervision.

Even though my life was going well, I still craved drugs. I married my high school sweetheart. After a few years and a couple of kids, we were able to build a beautiful house. Since my drug habit got expensive, I turned to using alcohol since it was cheaper and easier to obtain. I was not a very good husband to her, even though she was the love of my life, and I wanted her to be happy.

She was everything a man could want, beautiful, good mother, and seemed to be the perfect wife, or so I thought. I settled into a routine that was common amongst my friends. I spent most of my time on my job, but during my off-time, I was either playing golf or going hunting, and drinking alcohol of course.

My friends and I agreed that our wives were unreasonable in their requests to spend more time with them. It came as a crushing surprise to me when I found out that my wife was seeing other men. Not one man but a lot of men. I was so upset that I could barely stand the pain.

I did not ask for a divorce and my drinking increased. I began to simply survive from one day to another. I had to make a living, but it was hard to keep my mind on my job. All I thought about was my next drink. My boss began to notice and comment, but I was too engrossed in my feelings to care. I began to drink on the job, and I am sure that he knew it, but he never said anything to me. I could still function effectively. I had become a valuable asset and I knew it.

I did not understand my wife's behavior and how she could be so bold. She did not care what I thought and did not seem to care if the children knew about her affairs. Since I had been raised in a very moral household, her behavior was beyond anything I could have ever imagined.

Finally, after many arguments, my wife divorced me. She told me that she had never loved me. I allowed her to take everything we had worked to achieve because I still loved her and wanted the best for my children. My drinking increased, and when I could get my hands on some drugs, I added them to the mix.

My life began to come unglued. On my job, I could still read complex blueprints and supervise men while building multi-story buildings. The buildings always passed the building inspections. I convinced myself that I could think clearer when I had some alcohol on board. I am sure that this was the only reason my boss let me get away with drinking on the job. I was a functioning alcoholic who could still do my job.

My personal life went completely out-of-control. I was caught driving while drunk and got my first DUI. My mother helped me to resolve the legal aspects of the problem. However, since I lost my license, it became a problem about driving my truck. I had no choice but to drive it anyway. How was I to get to work or anywhere?

Life became very hard. I got two more DUI's and my mother always came to my rescue. She bailed me out and hired lawyers who got me off. She and my father had numerous arguments about it, but she came up with the money even though they had saved all of their lives for their retirement. I didn't care. I did not want to go to jail. So, in the early years of my addiction, I never served any time in jail due to my DUIs.

I needed alcohol because it became an obsession with me and helped me to cope with my miserable existence. I started to go to clubs where I met my second wife who was also an alcoholic.

By this time, my thinking had gotten so distorted I rationalized that we would be a good match. She would understand me. What I did not know was that I would not be able to understand her and put up with her alcoholism. I was a functioning alcoholic, but she was a non-functioning one.

She would get violent and wanted to fight when she got drunk. We got a divorce.

I went back to the clubs because it was a place where I was accepted, and nothing was expected of me. Finally, my boss began to lose patience with me since I would drive to the clubs with the back of my truck loaded with expensive tools, and they were stolen while I was getting drunk...time and again. He threatened to take the money out of my check, but he never did. He never threatened to fire me. I just chalked him up as being a grumpy old man that should be thankful that I was making him a lot of money.

In those days, there was only one thing that made me truly happy. I liked to hunt and belonged to a hunting club. I was surrounded by some buddies who understood me. While most of them were not full-blown alcoholics, most of them drank a lot of alcohol. It never dawned on me how dangerous it was to be in the woods with men who were drinking and carrying shotguns.

My hunting buddies lost patience with me one time when I drank myself into oblivion and threatened to whip all of their butts. I didn't even remember this incident and had to be told about what happened the next day. Cold-sober, it frightened me to think that if I was mad enough to physically whip my friends, I might have shot one of them. I was told that they had to call my father to come to the club and lead me out of the woods.

My life continued haphazardly until I met another woman who was also an alcoholic and a sorry individual to boot. It took me a while to figure that out. I was still living with my parents because I was not able to save up enough money to rent a place. My father was unhappy with two alcoholics in the house, but my mother kept making excuses for both of us, even though she did not care for my new wife. I was her baby boy, and she had to take care of me, or so it seemed. I took advantage of her love for me.

Due to a workman's compensation claim based on the accident, which was partially due to my drinking, I received a good settlement and bought a new truck. It didn't take but a few weeks before my new wife skipped town with it and with what little money I had leftover after I bought the truck. It put me back to driving my old jalopy truck. I was broke and still living with my parents.

My boss never fired me. Instead, he got sick and died, and his wife closed down the business. I had to find another job. Not long after that, my father died also. I kept getting DUIs, and my mother kept bailing me out. Finally, after about ten of them, my mother ran out of money, and I had to go to jail. It was the best thing that ever happened to me. They don't serve alcohol or drugs in jail. I finally got out after three years.

My mother is very sick, and I am trying to work and take care of her as best that I can. I am still living with her. She brags to everyone about how good I am to her. She is pretty much bed-ridden and requires a lot of care.

I have a sister who lives next door; however, she is also on drugs and does not help me take care of our mother. She is useless and has ruined her life. Now, cold-sober, I understand why my father got upset with both of us.

I have found a job in construction and am making a fair salary. Life is very hard, but I am off of alcohol and am thinking a lot clearer these days.

When I look back on my life, I wonder if anyone could have stopped me from becoming an addict. If my boss had fired me, I might have gotten the message that my drinking was ruining my life. But I am not sure that would have made me change my behavior. If my mother had not bailed me out so many times, I might have been sent to jail sooner. Becoming cold sober and being forced to follow some rules has done more for me than any other consequence that I have ever had to face in life.

The desire for alcohol and drugs still plagues me but I have managed to resist the temptation up to this point. However, I wonder how long I can hold out.

MARSHA'S STORY – AN ENABLER

I am the mother of an alcoholic. This is a story about Jessica, my daughter. I was a delighted woman the day she was born because I had birthed two boys ahead of her and was ready for a baby girl in my life.

Although her alcoholism has dramatically affected other members of the family, this is primarily a story about our relationship and how alcohol has impacted both of our lives. If someone had told me twenty years ago that I would be writing a story about Jessica being an alcoholic, I would have informed them that they were crazy.

As a small child, Jessica was a sweet and beautiful little girl who gave me no trouble. She had long, blond, curly hair and spent most of her time drawing, singing, and practicing her cheerleading moves.

I had no complaints about her behavior until she turned thirteen years old. At that time, her behavior changed dramatically, much like a light switch being flipped, and she became a highly rebellious teenager almost overnight. She did not drink alcohol or take drugs at that time but *acted out* and created problems that affected the entire family. She would sneak out of a window in the middle of the night, balked about doing anything she was asked to do, and ran away from home frequently.

My husband always avoided being a disciplinarian, so it was left up to me to deal with her bad behavior which made me the *villain* in the house. I became Enemy Number One. She began to hate me over simple instructions to clean her room, to do her homework, and to be home by a certain time. She would tell me, "You are not going to tell me what to do." She always got punished, but it never stopped her from misbehaving or making that statement.

Although her teenage years were difficult, we got through them, and she got married by the time she was eighteen years old. After she had left home, her behavior improved dramatically, and she stopped hating me. We became good friends. It was nice to have a pleasant relationship with her after all those tumultuous years.

During the early years of her marriage, she had two children, went to church regularly, was a very moral person, lived in a very expensive home, drove a sports car, and was married to someone who adored her. There were some problems in the marriage but life was good for her, and we remained friends.

She admitted to me once, "Mom, I try very hard to build up a situation, and then I lose my temper and tear it all down again." This was before she became an alcoholic. Now, since she is so far gone, I am not sure she even feels remorse for her actions anymore. She justifies her bad behavior by blaming others for causing her to lose her temper. I am the main one she blames.

In earlier years, before she started drinking, she tried to get help from several medical doctors to no avail. She wanted them to help her cope with her panic attacks and *bad nerves,* but none of them would treat her with medication, fearing that she would become a drug addict. Go figure!

This was one of the reasons she became an alcoholic. She knew she needed help but resisted seeking any psychiatric counseling because she refused to admit that she had any mental problems. She was just nervous she said.

Needing something to calm her nerves, she began to drink heavily at the age of 35 years old, and her life changed dramatically. She developed an out-of-control temper and alcohol exacerbated her ability to control her emotions. It was as if she had returned to being a teenager again. Her temper has created most of the chaos experienced in her life.

She divorced her first husband and began to frequent bars, stating that she found more friends there who accepted her than she had ever found in a church. She met and married a very nice guy that the whole family loved, but it did not last long. Her drinking increased which created problems in the marriage, and she divorced him. He was *too nice* she said and needed more of a challenge. As time went on, she began to drink Vodka around the clock and seven days a week.

Once again, I became Enemy Number One. No matter what happened to her, even if I had absolutely nothing to do with her problem, she somehow managed to turn it around and make it my fault. I have been blamed for every bad thing that has ever happened to her. She has told so many lies about me that she has begun to believe them herself, and this has turned into serious delusions in her mind.

She has confronted me about things that are made up in her mind; terrible things she claims that I have done to her. One delusion she argued with me about once was, "You choked me every day. I had to go to school with bruise marks on my neck, and I was embarrassed." This never happened. I have never choked anyone in my entire life and certainly have never choked her.

Jessica believes her delusions are correct and cannot be convinced otherwise. When you are giving 200% to help someone, and all they do is curse you, tell lies about you, and tells you what a horrible person you are, it destroys some love that you have for that person, even if it is your child.

My mental health started to deteriorate, and I became very depressed. It is said that suppressed anger causes depression. I had plenty to be angry about. My husband would not confront her. He even went so far as to handle some situations in such a way that made her think that he was taking up for her; pitting her against me which reinforced my *bad guy* reputation.

No matter how disrespectful she treated me, I went overboard to make sure she had everything she needed in life. I have often wondered where she would be now if I had stopped enabling her in the early years of her addiction. Maybe she would never have sunk as low as she has in life. I have constantly rescued her.

Why did I continue to enable her? She was my daughter, and I loved her, no matter what. What does any good mother do when her child needs help? The question is: What is the definition of help? I thought I was helping her and did not realize that I was hindering her from facing up to the consequences of her actions. Intellectually, I knew what an enabler was, but my heart got in the way of rational thinking.

My husband and I both came down with severe and terminal health problems. I don't remember her ever doing a single thing to help my husband and me through those difficult days. My husband died, and things got much worse for me. I miraculously survived and was forced to go back to work. Jessica had sunk so low that I had to take care of her by myself financially.

I provided an apartment for her to live in, paid her utilities, provided food, and gave her spending money. I was helping her, or so I thought. But was I helping her? She was not disabled, but she could not seem to take care of herself. She kept saying that she was looking for a job, but I am confident that she never tried very hard. Why should she make an effort? I provided her with a bed of roses.

Instead of trying to find a job and do right, she brought men into the apartment, fed them the food that I provided, and lived the high life while I worked hard on my job.

Now, when I look back over my actions, I cannot figure out how I could have been so ignorant. My only defense is that my own life was so hard that I was simply doing whatever it took to get from one day to the next.

I was plagued with financial problems because of my husband's untimely death, was working on my job under difficult situations, and was responsible for the care of a mother who had become bedridden, senile, and contrary.

My daughter's foolish behavior continued, and so did mine. When I could no longer afford an apartment for her, I brought her into my house, fed her, and gave her spending money. Whenever I was away for a day or two, staying at my mother's house, she would bring men into my house.

Some items were stolen during those times, whether by her or by one of the men, I will never know. We had arguments about this behavior, but her standard reply was "You are not going to tell me what to do." She would brag that *tough love* did not work on her.

I became desperate to get help for her. Over the years, once she agreed to go into a voluntary rehab-center, but by the few minutes it took for me to drive back home, she pulled a con-job on the director and pretended to go into delirium tremors and was sent to a hospital.

Another time, a pastor at a church paid for her to go into another rehab-facility. I spent $500 for clothes, shampoo, hairdryer, and more for her to use while she was staying there, but she only stayed a few days and left the facility walking and left most of her "stuff" behind.

After being an alcoholic for nearly ten years, Jessica would get violent and abuse me. Periodically, she would threaten to commit suicide. Something drastic had to be done.

Finally, I faced up to the fact that she was suffering from more than just alcoholism, so I went to the courts to have her committed temporarily to a mental facility for evaluation. She was picked up at her boyfriend's house and involuntarily taken to a mental facility. It was a facility that only evaluated a patient's status, and the patients only stayed for one week.

After a week, I met with the psychiatrist of the facility, and he emphatically argued with me that she was only an alcoholic. I argued back and insisted that they get a second opinion from an outside psychiatrist. They did so.

After she had stayed in there another week, the second psychiatrist diagnosed her as having a Borderline Personality

Disorder. However, I was informed that there was no medication or treatment for that disorder. She was discharged. Once again…no help.

By the time she was discharged, she had the staff members convinced that I was the one who needed treatment instead of her. Actually, at that time I probably could have used some help. I desperately needed treatment for my enabling/codependent personality. The only reason I did not take her home with me was that I was afraid for my life. Instead, she went back to her boyfriend's house. The boyfriend is/was a drug addict.

During the latter years that I provided care for Jessica, she lived downstairs in my house, and I lived upstairs. She hit me on a few occasions, once kicking me up the side of my head from the back seat of my car while I was trying to drive her to the hospital to undergo surgery. One time she knocked me out for a few seconds while I was driving in heavy traffic.

Her favorite thing to do was to curse me for everything that she could think of, tell me what a rotten mother I had always been, and finished it off by spitting in my face. Thankfully, her aim got worse, and I got quicker on my feet. Spitting in one's face is the ultimate degradation of another person is why she did it, knowing that it would hurt me to the core. My hide got thicker and thicker as time went on, but my stupidity continued.

After years of her abuse, I went to the courts and applied for a protective order to be placed against her. It took me almost a year to consider taking this action before I finally made up my mind to go through with it. This order put her out of the house, stopped her from harassing me, calling me to curse me out over the phone, and to stop her physical and mental abuse. This was one of the hardest things I have ever done, but it was one of the best things that I have ever done to preserve my sanity.

Life continued. I worried about her, but I had other problems to deal with and was relieved when I no longer had to deal with her crazy behavior. Once, despite the protection order, she showed back up at my house. My heart took over, and I offered for her to stay with me again. Love can make a person continue to act dim-witted against all rational reasoning. I told her, "You can stay here if you want to but you will have to stop drinking or make every effort to do so, and you cannot treat me like you have in the past."

Her immediate response to that statement was for her to get into a *fighting posture* and tell me once again, "You are not going to tell me what to do." Then she proceeded to come toward me menacingly. I had a glass of water in my hand and threw it on her which stopped her momentarily.

I managed to get her out of my house, using the threat of jail because of the protective order and put her back on the road again. Talking about these things does not come easy, and the memory of watching her walking down the street and away from my house, not knowing where she might go or what might happen to her, broke my heart into a million pieces.

She has been raped several times, lived in shacks in the woods, walked for miles to find a public bathroom that had a plug for her hairdryer, panhandled for money to buy food, and who knows what other un-Godly things she has resorted to surviving on the streets.

She confided in me once about some of the problems she encountered while living on the streets. I cannot imagine in my wildest dreams why she would continue to live in these miserable situations when I am capable of providing her with above-average living conditions. All I require is that she control her behavior. But she is so self-destructive, she refuses to follow any rules and try to live a healthy life.

Her miserable existence on the streets does not deter her from drinking alcohol. No matter how horrible her situation is, she always keeps herself clean, wears very stylish clothes that come from the Goodwill Store, and keeps her hair styled to perfection.

Being a beautiful woman, with a charming personality which comes and goes, works in her favor. She uses her looks and charm to manipulate people when it suits her, or when she wants something out of them. People will not hesitate to help her because she does not come across as a typical street person.

Her alcoholism has destroyed her health although there are few outward signs. She is constantly in and out of hospitals, primarily for pancreatitis from her alcoholism. Years ago, I heard a doctor tell her in one of her numerous hospital admissions that she would be dead in one year if she did not stop drinking due to the cirrhosis of her liver. Since then, she has developed diabetes since alcohol has affected her pancreas. The pancreas controls insulin production and manages it.

My daughter got so sick one time while living in another state; she came back home again because she was afraid she was going to die. For a change, she had a humble attitude. I agreed for her to stay knowing that once again, I was asking for trouble. She swore that she would treat me better than before when she had lived with me.

She lived up to her promise for a short while, and I enjoyed her staying with me. I fed her well and made sure she had all of her medications. Things were going better than usual, but it turned out that she had a warrant out for her arrest due to a misdemeanor charge for public drunkenness when she was living on the streets.

She was picked up from my house and taken to jail. I did not bail her out, not because I refused to do so, but because I simply did not have the money. Supporting myself and taking care of her for so many years had used up a lot of my money.

After she had gotten out of jail, she returned to my home for a short while. It wasn't long before she left and headed for the streets again. I live in a small town, and I think life is too boring in my community, and she seems to thrive on excitement, whether it is good or bad excitement.

She has bragged about how well she can survive on the streets and manipulate the system. It may sound weird, but I think this street-wise skill she has acquired has given her some measure of pride in accomplishment. It is too bad she cannot realize that pride in accomplishing a successful lifestyle is the greatest high one can achieve; far better than the high one gets from alcohol or drugs.

After all of these years, I have finally come to realize that my codependent personality has played a significant role in my daughter's addiction. However, I am through enabling her, but I am afraid that it is too late. She is so far gone in her addiction that it will take a miracle for God to turn her life around again.

I both want to see her, and I don't want to see her at the same time. In the meantime, I live in constant dread that I will receive a phone call that will inform me that my daughter is dead.

When I leave for work in the morning, and it is still dark outside, or when I return home after dark after an evening out, I am afraid that I will find her waiting for me on one of the patio couches downstairs, which has happened on several occasions. Every time a car slows down in front of my house, I cringe because I am afraid that she has returned home again. When she shows up, it means trouble for me. Big trouble! I fear that I will weaken and let her live with me again.

It is at times like this that my youngest daughter has been prompted to remind me about a snake story which goes like this:

A snake was crossing the highway and got run over by a car. A kind-hearted woman stopped to help the snake. It was still alive, so she took it home and nursed it back to health. One day, the snake bit her. Shocked, she asked the snake, "Why did you bite me?" The snake answered, "You knew that I was a snake. This is what snakes do, so why did you bring me to your home?"

When I waver about what I should do about my pitiful and homeless alcoholic daughter, my youngest one will say: "Remember the snake story Mom."

I have always been an emotionally strong person, but the thought of dealing with her out-of-control behavior again almost throws me into a panic attack. I even have difficulty praying for her anymore because I want to use denial and simply not think about her. Any memories I have of her usually make me remember the pandemonium that she has created in both of our lives. In spite of it all, I still love her, but I want to love her from a distance.

MARIE'S STORY - AN ADDICT

When her story began, Marie was an innocent, starry-eyed young woman who thought she was marrying the man of her dreams; a handsome, charming medical doctor. In her fantasy world, she was confident that they would live happily-ever-after. Her fantasy included a white house with a picket fence, and they would have children who would always adore her.

Her fantasy world started to come apart at the seams when she discovered that she was not the only one who adored her husband. His good looks, charm, and wit were also attractive to other women, and the temptation was too strong for her husband to resist. After many years of an unhappy marriage, they got a divorce.

Marie was a school teacher and had the means to support herself. For a long time, she was not interested in getting married again since she had become so disillusioned with her first marriage. Although she had always been a "social drinker," Marie began to drink more frequently. She was not the type to frequent bars and did her drinking in the privacy of her home. The alcohol helped to take away her emotional pain.

Still being relatively young and attractive, she met another man who wanted to marry her. Time had passed, and her hurt had subsided somewhat due to the influence the alcohol had on her brain. She thought that marriage would be different from the first one; besides, he was a good drinking buddy.

In the beginning, they were both heavy social drinkers, but as time went on they drank to excess, and Marie's personality began to change. She knew it but could not seem to control herself, or she simply did not care because she had slowly spiraled downward into alcoholism.

She continued to teach at school but never drank on the job. As soon as she got home, she would immediately start to drink, and instead of the alcohol making her feel better, she and her husband began to have serious arguments. Their marriage turned into a bitter battleground.

Not realizing how much Marie drank, her children blamed everything on her husband. She was too embarrassed to admit to her children that she and her husband were both drinking too much, and in her altered state of mind Marie also blamed him for most of their problems.

One day, being a knowledgeable person, she realized her life had turned into a nightmare. She did some serious self-evaluation; facing up to the fact that she had become an alcoholic. Although she had always been a strong person, the alcoholism had depleted her strong will. She needed help and told her husband, her drinking partner, her enabler, "You have got to do something with me. I need some help."

Her husband helped her make arrangements to enter a rehabilitation center where she resided for forty-five days. In the facility, she got the help she needed. She realized that her husband was "enabling" her by drinking with her and vise-versus. They were not good for each other.

In the facility, she contemplated whether she would have become an alcoholic if she had married a different man; one who did not drink, or was a mild social drinker, and if he might have put a stop to her excessive drinking before she became a full-blown alcoholic. There are no "do-overs" in life. She had to make the best of the rest of her life.

Post-rehab-facility, the mindset of the old Marie returned to guide her choices in life. Within a very short period, she divorced her drinking buddy. It had not been a marriage made in heaven from the start, and their drinking had formed the basis of a dysfunctional marriage.

Being naturally social-minded, she made a lot of good friends while she was in the rehab-facility, and after they were all discharged, they formed an informal support system for each other. They engaged in all types of fun events, including overnight trips out of town. She found out that she could have a good time without drinking alcohol.

However, she still had to attend AA meetings for over twenty-five years because the urge to drink still plagued her at times. She attended Al-Anon, and it helped her to see how her alcoholism had not only impacted her marriage and her life in general, but it had caused devastating effects on the lives of her family. This helped her to stay sober.

Being a charming and comely woman, once again, she met another man who wanted to marry her. He was not a drinker, and this marriage was more-or-less a marriage of convenience. It did not take her long to realize that they were not compatible with all of the ways that produce a happy marriage.

Marie was no longer the naive and innocent woman who had married her first husband. She had suffered a lot of bumps and bruises since that time in her life, and maybe some of her past experiences played a part in how she approached her third marriage. Nevertheless, she did not divorce her third husband.

Instead, they worked at the marriage and developed a comfortable relationship.

After many years of marriage, her husband contracted a terminal illness, and Marie helped him through this difficult period until his death. Once again, Marie was single.

Today, she is retired from teaching. She has not "fell off the wagon" since her stint in rehabilitation and lives an uncomplicated and relatively happy life. She plays bridge three times a week which keeps her mind sharp and lives in a quaint cottage on a street with some other widows who have befriended her. They are the "Merry Widows" of the Riverside Retirement Community who are always looking for something fun to do, even if it is only eating out at a good restaurant.

Now, her only companion is a small Shih Tzu dog who brings her both pleasure and frustration both at the same time, much like the way she sometimes felt when she was married.

SUSAN'S STORY - AN ENABLER

Susan could be the "poster child" for codependency. What she has gone through, and is still going through, would probably drive the average woman into a mental institution.

She got married when she was very young to a handsome guy in the Air Force. He intended to make the Air Force a career choice. They moved around a lot and during the first few years, they had two children.

In the beginning, Susan was happy, but her life soon made a wrong turn. Her husband became an alcoholic and Susan's life became unbearable. She had been raised in a very dysfunctional home with an alcoholic father, and she did not want to raise her children under similar circumstances. She did not stay in the marriage and enable her husband to continue to drink, which was a wise choice. However, there is much more to Susan's story.

She became an enabler later in her life, as you will see when you read further. She divorced her husband and moved back to her home town.

Being a very strong-willed woman, she got a job with a company and worked her way up to a management position. While she was working hard to support herself and her kids, it seemed like it was only overnight that her kids were nearly grown. Being so busy all of the time, it came as a shock to her when she found out that her teenage son, Tommy, had developed a substantial drinking problem. His sister Jennie ratted him out because she was concerned about his welfare.

Susan was devastated. She had a long hard talk with Tommy, and he promised to quit drinking. He lied. She had believed his lie. However, as time went on, it became evident that he was drinking regularly; however, he never appeared to be drunk.

Tommy graduated from high-school and got a good job at a local manufacturing plant. Within a couple of years, he got married to a good woman, and they started to have children.

As time went on it became apparent to Susan that he had finally turned into a full-blown alcoholic, and it nearly drove her crazy. He was a functioning alcoholic. He rarely got drunk, and outsiders could barely tell that he was even drinking. However, having always been a sweet person, his disposition changed, and his drinking impacted his wife and kids.

Although he had a good stable job, it didn't pay a lot, and his drinking put a dent in the household budget. Tommy and his wife were always running out of money. Susan always felt as if she had to come up with some money to bail them out of trouble (did she?) time and again, to keep them from being evicted and to buy groceries for them to eat.

Tommy would not listen to anyone about his alcoholism. Why? He would not admit that he was an alcoholic. Just when Susan thought she could not take any more hurt in watching her son being taken over by alcohol, he had a heart attack. He was in his early thirties. This put an additional burden on Susan, both financially and emotionally.

By this time, her daughter, Jennie, had gotten married, and she did not drink or take drugs. However, the man her daughter married was an alcoholic. He was also a functioning alcoholic and could hold down a job, but when he was home, he treated Jennie terribly. Susan not only had to worry about her daughter's mental health, but she had to bail them out of a lot of financial problems brought on by his alcoholism. Her daughter frequently tried to leave her husband, but he would always make promises that he would change his ways. Like Tommy, he was a liar, which most alcoholics learn to do.

Susan's two kids were always pulling (pulling vs volunteering?) her into their problematic lives. She had no life of her own. Working hard at her job, she spent the rest of her time trying to resolve some of Tommy and Jennie's problems.

The years passed, but the problems continued to plague Susan. Tommy had two more heart attacks and open-heart surgery. Did he stop drinking? No.

Tragedy struck again; her daughter, who was by then in her forties, had a major stroke that landed her in the hospital, and she had four more strokes while she was in the hospital. Miraculously, due to Susan's desperate cries out to God, her daughter survived all of them with a minimum amount of disabilities. Did her daughter's husband stop drinking? No.

As of this writing, both Tommy and Jennie's husband are still drinking and making life miserable not only for Susan but for their families.

If Susan had refused to financially bail out Tommy and his wife in the early years of marriage, would it have made an impact on Tommy? Would this have forced him to man-up and do whatever it took to take care of his family?

If Susan had refused to financially bail out Jennie and her husband when she realized that her son-in-law was an alcoholic, would this have made an impact on her son-in-law? Would this have forced Jennie to stop enabling her husband and allowing him to manipulate her?

Who knows? This is the core problem that an "enabler" faces when dealing with an addict; they cannot say "No" to anyone, especially a loved one. At this writing, Susan is still enabling her kids. Years have passed, and now the grandchildren are grown. Some of them have turned to drugs and alcohol, and she is "helping" them also.

Where will it all end with Susan? She is such a hard-core codependent enabler; it will probably not end until her life is over. Who will enable her kids and grandchildren then?

CHARLIE'S STORY – AN ADDICT

I am a recovering drug addict. I have never been interested in drinking alcohol to excess or taking any kind of drug besides cocaine. Cocaine has always been my drug-of-choice. There is nothing that can compare to the high that one can get a hit of coke. I would do anything to get the drug so that I could experience that glorious high. When I came down from the high and needed the drug, I would become violent and lose my temper. I have wasted a lot of good years acting like an idiot.

I am now in my forties and have lived with my grandparents for most of my life. My mother died when I was a young teenager, and I have never been close to my father. I was not on drugs in my teens. I graduated from high school and went to college for a short period. I got married and dropped out of college; however, I got a good job with a large company.

I loved my wife dearly and would do anything to make her happy. No matter how hard I tried, I never seemed to make her happy, and she started to run around on me. The marriage eventually ended in divorce. I have never been so unhappy in my life. She had been my world. During one of my extreme bouts of depression, someone offered me a hit of coke. My life changed dramatically from that time on. I found a way to ease the pain of losing my wife.

Due to my addiction that ensued from that first hit of coke, I eventually lost my job and was forced to move back in with my grandparents. They were very responsible people who loved me. I loved them in return.

However, as my addiction began to control my life, I became unbearable to live with due to my temper. I never hit my grandparents, but I knew my behavior upset them. I didn't care. I couldn't seem to help myself.

My grandmother would try to give me advice, but I would only chalk her up as being a nag. She was a feisty little old woman who sometimes came across as mean but had a heart of gold. I took advantage of her. In those days, I cared about what I was doing to her, but cocaine was running my life.

Over the years, I have honestly wanted to quit my drug addiction. I have been in and out of eight rehabilitation centers. While I was admitted, I would vow never to ingest cocaine again. As soon as I was discharged and returned home, the pressures of life would bear down on me, and I would start searching for the drug again.

In my wanderings around town, I met a woman called Rebecca. She was an alcoholic, and I brought her to live with me in my grandparent's house. My grandmother was not happy with my decision. It meant that she had to stretch the little money she had to feed another mouth. Rebecca did not work, primarily due to her alcoholic problem. Even though my grandmother grumbled and complained constantly, she stretched the money somehow.

I would pick up a couple of days of work here and there and bring home a few dollars. I would give my grandmother some of it, but before the sun went down, I would be demanding it back so that I could find some cocaine.

Rebecca and I always fought. This was distressing to my grandmother. I loved Rebecca, but we were not good for each other. While under the influence, we knew how to push each other's buttons. We would both become violent, and it is a wonder that one of us did not kill the other one.

My grandmother had to live through our battles. My grandfather died in the middle of my relationship with

Rebecca, and one might say that he just gave up and was glad to get out of the house, even going so far as dying to do so.

Once we fought and Rebecca pulled a knife on me. In my struggle to get it away from her, she accidentally sustained a cut on her hand. She called the police and placed all of the blame on me. I was arrested and taken to jail. Like most addicts, Rebecca could manipulate anyone into believing anything she said. My grandmother was a witness to what happened, but she still allowed Rebecca to stay in her home because Rebecca had nowhere else to go. Due to her alcoholism, she had alienated all of her friends and everyone in her family.

My grandmother made phone calls and spent money that she could not afford to get me out of jail. Knowing that Rebecca and I could not live under the same roof together after I returned to the home, my grandmother got up the courage to put Rebecca out of the house.

Time went on and I continued my drug habit even though I was continually drawn to God to change my ways. I tried to quit, but it would only last for a short period. Finally, my wake-up call came when my grandmother died. When she died, there was no one left on earth that would help me sustain my addiction. I was forced to get out and get a job to eat and put a roof over my head.

By divine intervention, I came into contact with a local pastor who became my mentor. Through the efforts of this minister, I am now recovering from my addiction. With his help, I have started a program for the homeless in my city. I conduct church meetings and try to find shelters for homeless people. A few of them are mentally ill, but most of them are victims of some addiction.

Since my brain has cleared up from the effects of cocaine, I have begun to realize how selfish I have been all of my life. My behavior has brought me nothing but misery, but now I feel good about myself since I am helping others.

Once, I ran into Rebecca on the streets and told her what I was doing; that I was a changed man. I offered to help her get into a rehab program, but she refused. The last time I saw her, she walked away from me and started down the street toward the center of the city, a place where she knew she could get someone to buy her some alcohol.

I still struggle with the craving for cocaine when things don't go well in my life, but I have managed to remain clean for two years. I regularly pray for God to help me because I cannot do it on my own.

GWEN'S STORY - AN ENABLER

On my wedding day, I was thrilled to be marrying a man that loved me and that I loved with all of my heart. He was handsome, intelligent, witty, charming, and I knew that he would be a great husband and a good provider. What else could I ask for in a spouse?

In the beginning, life was just as beautiful as I had envisioned it would be. We were both teachers and loved our jobs. Since we were both extroverts, we attracted a lot of friends. Everyone loved my husband because he was a witty and funny guy. We were not only married, but we were also best friends and had a lot of fun together.

I used to be a "social drinker," and only drank occasionally. However, my husband drank every day. He admitted to me that he had started drinking a lot while he was still in high school. From the very beginning of our marriage, he continued to drink every day.

In all the years of our marriage, I have never seen him drunk, even though he drank at least six beers or more every day. Maybe, it was because he stuck to drinking beer and never drank the hard liquor. Since he was never sloppy drunk, I was not overly concerned about his drinking. No one could tell that he was drinking, except it made him a little wittier and funnier.

We eventually had three children and continued to teach at the local schools. While I was satisfied with teaching in elementary school, my husband was ambitious and rose through the ranks to become the principal of a middle school. He loved it and never drank on the job.

As I look back on our lives, I now see that I enabled him to drink because I would buy the alcohol for him and place it in the refrigerator. I loved him, and I wanted to please him. We would entertain frequently, and I always secured the alcohol for the parties. Since my husband nor my friends acted inappropriately, I could see no harm in providing liquor for him or our friends.

However, when my husband retired, our lives began to fall apart. His drinking increased. He started to drink the hard stuff rather than sticking to beer. However, aside from him acting a little sillier when he was trying to be funny, he still did not exhibit signs of being a sloppy drunk. But things were just not quite right in our marriage. I wanted a sober husband.

He was not one for sitting around the house, so he got interested in playing tennis every day. While I liked to play tennis, I did not want to play as often as he did, so he went alone many times and picked up a partner to play with him in the tennis rounds.

That became his downfall; he picked up a lovely tennis partner who liked to play more than tennis. As far as I know, this was the first time that my husband strayed out of the bounds of our marriage.

When I became suspicious, I followed him one evening and found him with this other woman. When he got home, I confronted him, not only about the woman but about his excessive drinking. I felt as if he would not have done such a thing if he had been sober most of the time. I threatened to call our adult children. He begged me not to call them.

I was too angry to be reckoned with, so I called our children and told them what was going on. They were shocked. Although they were well aware of his excessive drinking, they were shocked to hear that their father had committed adultery. All of our children arrived at our home within a short period.

United, they injected themselves into the situation and convinced their father to change his ways. He had to promise to give up drinking entirely, give up the woman, and attend AA meetings for the rest of his life.

I don't think he would have listened to me if I had not brought the children into the situation, but from that "intervention" until he died thirteen years later, he attended AA meetings regularly, sometimes twice a day, and he never took another drink.

The last thirteen years of our lives together were fantastic, and I wish I had faced up to what his excessive drinking was doing to our marriage and confronted him a lot sooner.

TOM'S STORY – AN ADDICT

I am a recovering addict from being addicted to both alcohol and drugs. I am a registered nurse who has worked my way up to a supervisory position in a major hospital. I am interested in telling my story to show that it is possible to overcome addictions and put that life behind you. However, it is very hard. I still attend AA meetings regularly.

Twenty years ago, I was working as a registered nurse for another hospital. I had dabbled in drugs when I was a teenager but would not call myself a full-fledged addict. However, when I began to work around drugs as a registered nurse, the enticement to take some drugs without permission was an overwhelming temptation.

At first, I only took a few of the drugs that I found in the patient's medication drawers that were not considered to be *controlled substances*. Some of these same drugs today are locked away in a controlled drug box that takes two nurses present for it to be opened. Time went on, and I needed drugs that would give me a bigger high. I convinced myself that being a nurse was stressful and that I needed them to get through the day.

Finally, I was caught and reprimanded but not fired. I stopped for a little while, but then I began to take the drugs again. I was caught again and given a choice of being fired or going to a rehabilitation center. I chose rehab. While there, I listened to the advice they gave us, participated in all of the programs, and vowed to quit taking drugs.

When I got out and started working for the hospital again, I started to drink alcohol when I was off duty. Alcohol was cheaper and easier to obtain. The only problem with drinking alcohol and trying to work was that people could smell it on my breath. With drugs, unless I was extremely high, no one was the wiser.

Not being able to drink and work, I started to take the drugs again. This time, I was more careful. Nevertheless, I got caught again. Once more, they gave me the option of being fired or going to rehab again. I wondered how they could be so stupid. Even though I chose rehabilitation, I was not in a cooperative frame of mind. However, I did not want to get fired and did not have a choice in the matter.

After admission to a different rehab, this time something clicked in my head, and I truly listened and participated in the programs offered at the center. Somehow, I got it through my hard head that this was my last chance to change, or my registered nurse's license would be suspended, and nobody would hire me. I had spent four years earning my degree, and I was in danger of throwing my career away.

When I got out at that time, I went back to work for the hospital and never turned back to drugs or alcohol. I began to go to AA meetings, frequently. As time went on and other nurses began to have drug and alcohol problems, I started a support group that was sanctioned by the administrator of the hospital.

Now, after twenty years, the only time I think of drugs or alcohol is when I have mowed my lawn on a hot day and think about how good a cold beer would taste.

BEATRICE'S STORY – AN ENABLER

Beatrice was a very quiet, introverted woman who came across as a "wimp" who had no backbone. However, that was not so. She endured more than the average woman could tolerate and did so without whining.

Her husband, Sam, was a very charming person that everyone liked. Sam was a good man when he wasn't drinking. He loved his kids: three girls and one boy. They lived modestly, mostly on small farms where Sam could raise food for the family. However, they moved a lot.

Beatrice had a brother, but they did not communicate with each other often. On the other hand, Sam was one of six brothers and sisters. His parents lived on a farm, and they all got together regularly. They were a close bunch and liked to have fun. While their mother cooked big meals for the entire family to enjoy, the rest of the family all gathered in the yard to play baseball or volleyball.

While Sam, his children, and the rest of the family played, Beatrice kept to herself, and this caused the others to judge her harshly. His brothers and sisters talked behind her back and decided that Sam was unhappily married to Beatrice.

What they didn't know was what truly went on in the marriage. Sam was a binge alcoholic. His behavior contributed to Beatrice's state of mind and her behavior.

Sam had a good job and only farmed to help out with the household budget. Since he was raised on a farm, it was in his blood. He never drank on his regular job, but as soon as Friday and payday came around, Beatrice knew what was going to happen. It happened every Friday.

After he got paid, he would not go straight home from work; instead, he would go to a local illegal gambling establishment to start drinking and playing poker.

Many times, when he got home, he would collapse in the middle of the floor, promptly vomiting on himself and the floor. While he was passed out, Beatrice learned to search his pockets for some money to pay the bills and buy a few groceries. Sometimes she found some and sometimes not.

With the assistance of the kids, Beatrice would get Sam up from the floor and put him in his bed. Beatrice would clean him up and put some clean pajamas on him. Then she would clean up the floor.

The next morning, Sam would wake up and find himself in a clean bed with clean clothes on. He had no recollection of how he got there. The sun would be coming up, and everything seemed fine, except for a slight hangover. He would remember some things that had transpired the night before, but he could not remember whether he had won or lost at poker. The next Friday, he would repeat this destructive cycle, Friday after Friday.

Should Beatrice have left him in the middle of the floor, lying in his vomit, so that he would wake up the next morning in this terrible state? Sam was not the best husband in the world, but Beatrice loved him. Would you let someone you love to sleep all night in the middle of the floor lying in vomit?

In the early years of their marriage, Beatrice had confronted Sam about his drinking and gambling, to no avail. She had no job skills that would allow her to divorce him, and he knew it, so she was trapped. Finally, she just gave up and accepted her fate in life. The problem was, the children suffered because his drinking and gambling caused them to live in poverty, and this made an indelible mark on their lives.

RACHAEL'S STORY – AN ADDICT

As I write this, I am sitting on the floor of an overcrowded jail cell. There is only room in here for four inmates, but there are seven of us in here. I am sleeping on the floor because I do not have a bunk bed. How did I get here?

I guess you might say I have been a rebel most of my life. I did not start drinking seriously until I was divorced from my first husband but my rebellious ways began when I was a teenager. I ran away from home numerous times. I would go out a window at night to go partying and would resist all rules and regulations. However, I graduated from high school only because my mother pushed me.

To get back at her, I refused to ride the school bus. I would hitch-hike my way to school and back which drove my mother crazy. It still drives her crazy. I have hitch-hiked to Chicago, to San Francisco, to Miami and all over the country. My favorite place to visit is Little Rock, Arkansas.

My mother and I always fought when I was a teenager. She is the meanest woman in the world. She never tires of trying to control me. She nagged at me to clean my room, help around the house, do my homework, stop running away from home, be back home on time when I went out, and various other stupid rules that I considered to be unreasonable.

We still fight about the same things. Although I am now in my 40's, I live with her off and on because my alcoholism has hindered my ability to hold down a job so that I can provide a roof over my head. She always claims that she is helping me, but all I can see is that she is trying to control me.

She refuses to bail me out of jail this time claiming that she is through with me. I am her daughter. Who deserts their daughter? Even if this is my third time to be incarcerated for public drunkenness and minor theft, she needs to stand by me. I am not in here for doing something God-awful like murdering somebody or robbing a bank.

Once, I had just been released from the hospital after many admissions to be detoxed, and my mother would not come and get me. I didn't have any money, and all I wanted from Wal-Mart was some hair spray. I am funny about my hair. I am obsessed with my hair looking nice, my clothes too. They had me arrested even though they could see that I was drunk and did not know what I was doing. I still had the hospital band on, but they would not listen to reason.

I am in jail with a bunch of losers. They drive me crazy with their loud talking, fighting, and horrible manners. A lot of them are lesbians and do not care who watches them in their sexual encounters. It is like being in a cage with a bunch of wild animals.

My mother claims that she worries about me, but she is just a control freak. I have told her time and again that I am a grown woman, and she cannot tell me what to do. I can do anything I want to do when I get out of this jail cell. I don't tell my boys what to do. I haven't seen either one of them in years. They are successful I am told. I let their father take custody of them when they were teenagers. I hated to let that SOB have them, but I didn't feel as if I had any choice. I didn't want them to grow up and hate me like I hate my mother.

Since my mother or no one else in my family will help me, I guess I need to make some plans for when I get out of here next week. Maybe I will hitch-hike back to Little Rock.

Although I hate my mother, I write lots of letters. I need her to put money on my account here in jail. She is such a sucker; she believes anything that I say.

MICHAEL'S STORY – AN ENABLER

I am the father of a drug addict. Ironically, I am also a bail bondsman who has arrested thousands of people, some are alcoholic or drug addicts who have skipped out on the bail that I provided for them while they waited for their court date. I make very good money in my profession, and I own some other businesses. I provide well for my family.

I have four boys of my own, and I never dreamed that anyone of them might ever turn to drugs. I am a very tall and large, not fat, man who usually intimidates people simply by my size. It has always worked for me in my business.

Not bragging but I am considered to be a good-looking man. When I go to pick up someone who has jumped bail, I dress up in an expensive black suit which makes me look rather sophisticated. I have never understood why people are less afraid of a nice-looking man than they are of an ugly one. Go figure! However, it works for me and allows me access to people's homes more readily so that I can pick up the individual who has jumped bail.

Somehow, since I had always been so successful in intimidating people, I convinced myself that my boys would be too scared of me to do anything illegal. I was wrong. With my past experiences with drug addicts, one might think that I would have recognized the symptoms exhibited by my oldest son after he started taking drugs.

However, it was not until some of my money came up missing that I began to wonder what was going on. At first, I thought that maybe I was getting forgetful, even though I am only in my forties, and simply did not remember spending the money.

Finally, another one of my sons came to me and snitched on his brother. I was shocked and confronted my son who was the addict. Of course, he denied everything and called his brother a liar. This was only the beginning of the chaos he began to create in the family by his manipulative and lying behavior.

Like many parents who love their children, my wife and I went along with some of his dysfunctional behavior, tried to help him in every way that we could, to no avail. Soon, he could not cover his drug habit due to his out-of-control behavior.

I started to suspect him of stealing some more money from me and decided to trap him. After counting the money in my coat pocket, I hung it in my usual place on the coat rack just inside my closet. He did not realize that I had set a trap and sneaked into my bedroom where he helped himself to some of my money. Soon after, he left the house.

Immediately, I went to the closet and found that he had taken one hundred dollars. I confronted him the next day, and he denied it as usual. Anger, hurt, and disappointment welled up in my throat. I told him how I had set a trap for him. To my amazement, he still venomously denied my accusations.

My first inclination was not to take a firm stand with him. I look back on that decision, and I wonder what I was thinking. Instead, I went to the hardware store and bought a deadbolt lock for my bedroom door. It was only when I got back and was installing it that it suddenly dawned on me as to what I was doing.

I talked with my wife and his three brothers, and I made a plan. My son owned all of the latest electronic gadgets and drove a brand-new truck. I took it all away from him. He blew up and started to shout at me. We got into an intense argument. I gave him a choice of changing his ways or leaving my house. He chose to leave.

As he walked out of my house and down the walkway, carrying two suitcases, I was tempted to call him back. My heart was breaking, but I knew that I was doing the right thing. Against my wishes, my mother took him in to live in her house. I was not happy about her decision because I am confident that my son is going to manipulate her and that she will enable him.

My mother's well-meaning efforts will hinder my son from facing up to his drug addiction. This is a story in progress and only time will tell how it will turn out.

MATT'S STORY – AN ADDICT

As a child, I was happy. Although I had a chaotic home life, I cannot blame my addiction on my parents or the way they raised me. My problem with drugs started in high school when I was introduced to them by one of my friends. Everyone was taking drugs, and I wanted to fit in with the crowd. Besides, I was curious as to how drugs would affect me.

From as far back as I can remember, I was a *star* in my family. My father enrolled me in little league at an early age, and it wasn't long before it was evident that I had an unusual ability to play baseball. Over the years, as I grew up, I took my star status for granted. It never dawned on me that I might one day lose everyone's respect.

When I first started taking drugs, I took them infrequently. I began running with the wrong but popular crowd, and I started taking the drugs more often. I managed to get a full-ride scholarship to college due to my athletic abilities. Everyone in the family was thrilled for me. By this time, I was taking drugs frequently but did not become an out and out addict until after I got married.

I couldn't wait to go to college. It was predicted that I would eventually end up in the major leagues. When I arrived at college, I was immediately drawn into a popular crowd.

I met a beautiful girl who had recently won a beauty contest in her state. We started dating and became close…too close. One day, she informed me that she was pregnant. Since she did not have a mother or any family member who could support her through the pregnancy, I felt as if I needed to drop out of college, get a job, and marry her. Besides, I loved her.

Returning home, I married her, and we moved in with my parents. This was a mistake. My wife and my mother did not get along very well, and my marriage started to unravel.

I got a well-paying job and finally saved enough money to rent a place. Our baby was born, and it was a boy. I loved him on sight and vowed to be the best father in the world.

I was working twelve to fourteen hours a day, making good money, but the minute I walked in the door my wife expected me to start taking care of the baby and doing things around the house. She did not work outside the home, and she didn't cook or clean the house. Things started to go sour.

On my job, I worked with a lot of men who took drugs, so supply was always readily available. Since my marriage was unraveling and my job was stressful due to the competitive nature of the business, I started to take more drugs than I had ever taken before. This added to the problems in my marriage.

Finally, my wife decided to leave me and go back to her hometown which was about a four-hour drive from where we were currently living. I didn't care that she was divorcing me, but it would mean that I would have to drive four hours one way to see my son.

She filed for divorce when she got home. I didn't know anything about divorce proceedings since none of my close relatives had ever gotten a divorce. She went to court, and I did not show up for the court date. I thought the judge would be fair and do the right thing by both of us. Just how stupid can a guy be?

Almost immediately after the divorce was final, I lost my well-paying job, and I had to take one that did not pay much over the minimum wage. My child support payments were based on my well-paying job. I didn't have the money to hire a lawyer to go back to court.

I moved back into my parent's home so that I could pay the child support the judge had set forth for me. When I found myself living a miserable life, I began to take more and more drugs.

My parents finally caught up with me. My father, who was not a full-blown addict but had dabbled in drugs since he was a teenager, did not take my drug addiction seriously. My mother, who was addicted to prescription drugs, did not help me. I wanted one of them to take charge and help me get off of drugs. However, there were a lot of problems going on in my parent's lives, and they were dealing with their demons that they could not seem to control. They accused me of adding to their problems.

Finally, my need for drugs became an overwhelming obsession, and I did not care what my drug addiction was doing to anyone. I needed the drugs, and that was all that I could think about day and night.

Life became much more complicated over the next couple of years, due to my drug addiction and my crazy ex-wife. We tried to reconcile several times, but it never worked. While my ex-wife is not an addict, she is severely dysfunctional, primarily due to her being raised by a mother who has a severe drug problem herself and goes in and out of jail and rehabilitation centers.

Finally, after I stole from my parents and created extreme pandemonium in their lives, my mother called my grandmother, and we all met at a doctor's office that treats drug addicts. I am now taking a drug, prescribed by a physician, which is supposed to help me to get off of my drug-of-choice which is OxyContin. He prescribed Suboxone.

As per **www.psychcentral.com**: *"When a 'partial opioid' like Suboxone is taken, the person may feel a very slight pleasurable sensation, but most people report that they just feel "normal" or "more energized" during medication-assisted treatment. If they are having pain, they will notice some partial pain relief.*

People who are opioid dependent do not get a euphoric effect or feel high when they take buprenorphine properly. Buprenorphine tricks the brain into thinking that a full opioid like oxycodone or heroin is in the lock, and this suppresses the withdrawal symptoms and cravings associated with that problem opioid."

Today, with the help of the drugs prescribed by the doctor, I have a decent job and am off OxyContin. However, I am still living with my parents so that my mother can help me with my son when I bring him home every other weekend. He is a bright spot in my life. I have not had many bright spots since I fell from grace as the *star* of my family.

Up-date to this story: My miserable life continued until I moved to another city where I met a good woman. I continued to take Suboxone for several years. However, when my new wife told me that she was pregnant and it was another son, I gathered up my Suboxone and flushed it down the toilet. I finally decided that I needed to be a healthy, drug-free father to my kids.

CONNIE'S STORY – AN ENABLER

This story will be different than the other stories in this book, dealing with what most people think of as "enabling" behavior - actions that are harmful when dealing with an addict. There are many forms of "enabling." Not helping a person but simply not doing anything to stop bad behavior can enable someone to continue engaging in destructive behavior. This is a story of such a woman.

I am confident that no one will recognize my story as being about Mack and me because we both put up a "fake" front to our friends and our neighbors. He put up a front as being a great guy, while I put up a front as being a happy wife married to a great guy. Nothing could have been further from the truth.

When we were dating, I discovered that my husband drank a lot with his friends, but I thought drinking with his buddies was just something that young guys did during their rebellious teen years as they transitioned into adulthood.

Up until that time, the only person that I knew who frequently drank to excess was our next-door neighbor. He was a functioning alcoholic in that he could hold down a job, but "acted out" when he was home and under the influence of alcohol.

Neither one of my parents drank alcohol to excess and only drank socially occasionally, so I did not know much about the evils of drinking when I started going out with Mack. After a long, tumultuous period of dating, we decided to get married.

I couldn't understand why my neighbor's wife put up with his behavior. After marrying someone who also drank to excess, I was soon introduced to the same type of treatment as my neighbor's wife and began to slowly understand her response to her husband's drinking.

www.ncadv.org/images/Domestic%20Violence.pdf:

In the United States, an average of 20 people are physically abused by intimate partners every minute. This equates to more than 10 million abuse victims annually.

Domestic violence is prevalent in every community and affects all people regardless of age, socio-economic status, sexual orientation, gender, race, religion, or nationality. Physical violence is often accompanied by emotionally abusive and controlling behavior as part of a much larger, systematic pattern of dominance and control. Domestic violence can result in physical injury, psychological trauma, and even death. The devastating consequences of domestic violence can cross generations and last a lifetime.

Having almost no experience with alcoholism, I stayed in a state of anxiety. When my husband was not drinking, he could be charming and sweet, but as soon as he got a few drinks on board, his personality would change and I began to worry about what would happen next.

https://www.healthyplace.com/abuse/transcripts/emotionally-abused-women

There are many types of emotional abuse but most is done in an attempt to control or subjugate another person. Emotional abuse is like brainwashing in that it systematically wears away at the victim's self-confidence, sense of self, trust in her perceptions and self-concept.

Having no experience with alcohol and being so young, I allowed my husband to blame me for everything wrong in his life. Instead of confronting him, I began to work harder to please him.

As I look back at my neighbor's behavior, I now see his wife as an "enabler," who was a crabby woman, and I also understand why his children were insecure, defensive, and seemed unhappy most of the time.

It was only after we were married that I found out my husband drank a lot, seven days a week, and 365 days a year. Every afternoon, he would bring home at least a six-pack of beer, and he would drink a case of beer over the weekend. Thankfully, he always brought the beer home, rarely drank hard liquor, and did not stop off at bars.

This was one reason I cut him so much slack with his drinking at first. I didn't think he had a serious problem with alcohol because he was a person who could "hold his liquor." Since he never showed outward signs of being intoxicated, only that he got grumpy, I didn't blame our problems on alcohol. I allowed him to blame me. Stupid me!

It was as if he had a dual personality. The more he drank, the more it brought out his "dark side."

Most people viewed me as being a healthy, happy person. I was always smiling and trying to put my best foot forward. I planned all types of outings for the family and cooked giant meals for the holidays. From the outside looking in, nothing seemed amiss.

However, my children were aware that everything was not quite right in our "pretend paradise," I would infrequently lash out at my husband and the children didn't understand. It made me look bad. My husband would only "smirk" at how I had made a fool of myself.

The reader might wonder at this point why I continued to live in such a terrible state of anxiety. I became very depressed, and when you are depressed, you cannot think straight. I became paralyzed to do something constructive to improve my life and began to be plagued with thoughts of suicide which envelops you in a black cloud of hopelessness.

From this point on in my story, I'm going to leave out the bulk of my tale of woe, because as bad as it was up to this point...it got much worse over the years, and I got more depressed.

God must have taken pity on me because one day out of the blue, I suddenly "woke up" to what was happening, and I was able to see what part I was playing in making my own life miserable. I found myself at a turning point in my life; to work to regain control of my pitiful life.

For the first time in years, I was able to ignore Mack and began to make plans to get my life in order. Since I had invested a lot of time and effort in building a life, pretend life or not, which included a house and other material possessions, I did not want to give them up. I knew a divorce would not end my miserable relationship with Mack since we had kids; it would create more problems for me.

Sadly, as I slowly returned to my "sane" pre-marriage state-of-mind, my teenage children began to "act out."

No surprise that Mack refused to help me discipline them, and worked hard to be the "favorite parent." Since I had to be the disciplinarian, it wasn't hard for him to make me out as the "bad parent."

I decided to return to college to obtain a degree so that I would be able to get a job that paid well enough to support myself and my children and divorce Mack if it became necessary.

My husband was vehemently against me going back to college, but at this point in life, I didn't care what he thought. Going back to college was one of the best decisions I have ever made in my life. I made friends, made good grades, and eventually regained my self-esteem.

However, I was presented with more problems due to raising my family while going to college at the same time. By the grace of God, I managed to make it work. Mack did absolutely nothing to help me.

After graduation and having regained my independent nature, Mack began to treat me much better. I made it plain that he had lost control over me and that nothing he could do or say would ever bother me again. As the years passed, my husband's personality improved a lot, and he spent less time brooding and sulking. He slowed down on his drinking, and we lived out a few more decades in relative peace.

Mack has passed away at this writing, and I have often wondered how my marriage and life might have turned out if there had been no alcohol involved in our marriage. To this day, I still live with the wounds of that marriage. I bristle at the least little criticism that comes my way.

I am now married to a wonderful man who treats me extremely well. Finally, I am at peace with the world.

Remember: **Doing nothing** is a form of "enabling" in that it allows an abuser to continue to abuse you.

PAULA'S STORY – AN ADDICT

I am the sister of Josh, the man in the first story of this book. Although we grew up in church and had great parents, it didn't stop either Josh or me from turning to drugs. My story is different from Josh's story, in that I did not become an addict until I was grown. He began to experiment when he was a teenager like most addicts.

I wanted to make something of myself and went to college to become a nurse. When I graduated from nursing college as a registered nurse, I was excited to begin my career in the surgical department of a local hospital.

It was an exciting place to work although it was stressful due to the pressure put on me by the administration and the doctors. They expected me to be perfect, read every physician's mind, know exactly what tools and supplies he would need, understand what he/she was doing or going to do during the operation, even if I had never scrubbed in on an operation of that kind. I worked hard to please everyone.

About a year after graduating from college, I thought I was the luckiest girl in the world when I met my husband-to-be who worked as a chemical engineer in a local plant. He made good money, and we quickly began to accumulate some coveted material possessions including a nice house that we built next to my parents. At the time, I thought it was a good decision to live next door to my parents because I would be close in case they got sick and would need some help.

It didn't take long before I became disappointed in my marriage. My husband was a genius, truly a genius, but he was boring. This apathy toward my marriage and the stress on my job caused me to become depressed.

One day, one of the anesthetists left his bag of drugs in one of the surgical suites to go and talk to the charge nurse. I was cleaning instruments from the last case when I noticed his anesthetist's case. Right on top was some drugs in plain sight. I reached down and chose one of them and pocketed it. This was the initial beginning of my downfall and road to becoming an addict.

After being caught three times, sent to a rehabilitation facility paid for by the hospital, it didn't help me; I finally lost my nurse's license and was fired. Almost simultaneously, my husband divorced me. I didn't care.

While I was in one of the rehabilitation facilities, I met and married a man I had met there. After we got married, he stayed clean. I didn't. I was hired to do some odd jobs but lost them soon to my addiction.

My husband was a good man, but he put up with a lot from me. We had a son together, and he worked to be a good father. Having been an addict himself, he knew what I was going through and gave me too much leeway.

He died an early death in his forties, due to the abuse of the drugs he had taken years earlier. I didn't know what I was going to do; he had always taken care of our son and me. I never held a job very long.

My mother and father pitched in to provide food and other necessities for my son and me. I continued taking drugs. My father died and left the care of my mother to me; she was terminally ill from Parkinson's disease. Thankfully, Josh was released from prison about that time.

Without hesitation, he immediately jumped in to take care of our mother. We argued a lot about who should do what in caring for her. A small part of me knew that I was doing my mother wrong by not helping as I should. She always took care of me, but somehow, I couldn't seem to care. I was disappointed that Josh, of all people, could not understand how I felt. All I cared about was my next fix. Surely, he knew what that was like when he was an addict himself.

My mother died in her home with Josh continuing to help her until the very end. In some ways, I think it was a blessing for her to die. It was a blessing to me because it relieved me of guilt, knowing how I had disappointed her most of my adult life.

Although I am drugged out, I am aware that I have ruined my life and my son's life; however, being honest, I only care about getting some money to buy drugs. I don't know what will eventually happen to my son or me, but I don't seem to care anymore. Maybe Josh will take care of us.

My days mesh into another day in a blurred haze of hallucinations and the overwhelming desire to obtain more drugs.

EPILOGUE

I hope that the reader has learned something about addictions by absorbing the medical information but also through reading the "true stories" of both addicts and enablers.

If this book has been purchased, I assume the reader is looking for answers to help them understand an addict in their life and how to deal with them. All of the stories are different but they all have the same underlying themes.

After someone becomes a full-blown addict, they are no longer capable of understanding how their behavior can hurt others. Sometimes, it appears they don't care and it is hard for an enabler to understand. An addict's thoughts are consumed with getting the next fix.

The enabler cannot understand how helping someone, especially someone they love can be harmful behavior. They don't realize that change in behavior is only brought about by suffering from the consequences of wrong choices. Standing up under the pressures of life builds strength of character and self-esteem in an addict. Being too kind, helping too much, and enabling an addict hinders their ability to become a mature, responsible person.

HELPFUL WEBSITES TO RESEARCH:

More can be learned about addictions and codependency by visiting the following websites. Click on links below even though they are black and white

www.wikipedia.com

www.asamcriteria.org

www.alcoholrehab.com

www.psychcentral.com

www.venturarecoverycenter.com/drugs-alcohol-affect-brain

www.coda.org

www.al-anon.alateen.org/about-group-meetings

www.nar-anon.org

www.aa.org

www.na.org

www.merriam-webster.com

If links don't work, copy and paste into your browser.

Some of these links to the websites listed will work if this book is being read on a device that will allow the reader to access the Internet. However, it is also in paperback form.

There are many good books written by other authors on this subject.

OTHER BOOKS WRITTEN
BY
AUDREY PHILLIPS COX

All books are available in PB and ebooks on Amazon.com and other online bookstores. Some can be ordered through brick and mortar stores.

A PERSONAL JOURNEY INTO THE WORLD OF ALZHEIMERS–A true story about my best friend who came down with Alzheimer's at the early age of 50 years old. I tell you about our friendship before she came down with the disease, then I explain what happened afterward. I include medical information and explain the stages of the diseases. I stress the importance of being a caretaker. Her husband was her caretaker for 17 years and she died at home.

ABSOLUTE PROOF THAT GOD REALLY EXISTS – The first one-half of this book explains how God created the earth and discredits the nay-sayers and atheists. The last one-half is about how churches need to operate according to the will of God. Members of a church should act like Christians and not gossip and back-bite other members. All members should be friendly, encourage new and old members, and much more. Many years ago, as the author of the book, I had a *personal experience* where I now have absolute proof that God is real. Read about the event and decide for yourself.

HURRICANE SLAMS HOSPITAL – This is a story based very loosely on true events when a real hurricane hit a hospital I was working in at the time. It is a drama, but it is heavily infused with some quirky characters. These characters lend comedic relief to the horrific event. It is both a comedy and a drama. It has been said that a reader will not be able to lay down the book once they start to read it.

A SPECIAL CHRISTMAS STORY – This is a book with the plot set in 1948 and is about a 10-year-old girl who lives under "old fashioned" values. Hopefully, the young reader will subliminally incorporate some of these values into their thinking and their approach to life. It was the "good ole days."

UNDERSTANDING YOUR FICO CREDIT SCORE - This is a book that will help the reader to understand how the credit bureaus come up with a person's FICO score. By understanding what criteria they use, it will help the reader to improve their score.

BUBBLES THE LOVEABLE SEA MONSTER – Available only on Kindle. It is a children's book that teaches children about keeping our environment clean, especially the waterways. It is told in an entertaining style.

THE DEACON – This book is about an overly ambitious Christian man who married his high school sweetheart. Together, they worked extremely hard to achieve a successful life and vowed to overcome the racist image of being born black. Up until he was elected as a deacon of a predominantly white church, he lived a blessed life as a lawyer and her as a real estate broker. He gave God the credit. However, fate played a dirty trick on him. Through no fault of his own, he found himself in danger of losing everything both him and his wife had worked for all their life. They were in danger of financial ruin and ruining the lives of his loved ones as well. He made some bad choices that led to other bad choices until he found himself suffering from the Domino effect: One small change can eventually cause all the dominoes to fall.

There are questions at the end of the book to answer which would make the book an ideal choice for a Christian book club.

"When I sit down to write a book, I do not say to myself, I am going to produce a work of art. I write it because there is some lie that I want to expose, some fact to which I want to draw attention, and my initial concern is to get a hearing."

-George Orwell-

I work hard to write my books and
will appreciate a review when you read this book.
Thanks in advance!

Audrey Phillips Cox

Links:

www.apc-writer.com
for more info on books, blogs, and articles

www.amazon.com/author/apc-writer
to purchase a book or leave a review.

Made in the USA
Columbia, SC
29 July 2023

21014851R00061